Living through American History

Living through the
GREAT DEPRESSION

by Grace Hansen

WELCOME TO DiscoverRoo!

popbooksonline.com/grt-dep-life

abdobooks.com

Published by Pop!, a division of ABDO, PO Box 398166, Minneapolis, Minnesota 55439. Copyright © 2024 by Abdo Consulting Group, Inc. International copyrights reserved in all countries. No part of this book may be reproduced in any form without written permission from the publisher. DiscoverRoo™ is a trademark and logo of Pop!.

Printed in the United States of America, North Mankato, Minnesota.
052023
092023

Cover Photo: Getty Images
Interior Photos: Getty Images; Library of Congress
Editor: Elizabeth Andrews
Series Designer: Laura Graphenteen; Neil Klinepier

Library of Congress Control Number: 2022950517

Publisher's Cataloging-in-Publication Data
Names: Hansen, Grace, author.
Title: Living through the Great Depression / by Grace Hansen
Description: Minneapolis, Minnesota : Pop!, 2024 | Series: Living through American history | Includes online resources and index
Identifiers: ISBN 9781098244316 (lib. bdg.) | ISBN 9781098245016 (ebook)
Subjects: LCSH: Great Depression, 1929--Juvenile literature. | Economic history--Juvenile literature. | United States--Juvenile literature. | Social history--Juvenile literature.
Classification: DDC 973.2--dc23

*Scanning QR codes requires a web-enabled smart device with a QR code reader app and a camera.

TABLE OF CONTENTS

CHAPTER 1

THE GREAT CRASH

In 1928, the future seemed bright for those living in the United States. But several issues would quickly lead to a historic **economic** crash.

Unemployment was becoming a problem. Factories were creating

products faster and better. New methods

required skilled labor, which led to

unskilled workers losing their jobs.

US farmers were suffering too. During World War I, the United States **exported** many of its goods to Europe. Some farmers borrowed money to buy more land and keep up with demand. But when World War I ended, Europe did not need US products anymore. Farmers could no longer pay their **loans**. They lost their land.

On Tuesday October 29, 1929, American investors and shareholders lost approximately $25 billion in the **stock market** crash. This day became known as Black Tuesday.

CHAPTER 2

NO JOBS

By 1932, the United States was in the middle of the Great Depression. Many factories shut down. Unemployment had risen from 8.7% in 1930 to 23.6%. Those who managed to keep their jobs often had to work for less pay. Children

sometimes dropped out of school to work.

Black Americans had an even more difficult time finding work due to **discrimination**.

Two men in Chicago, Illinois, show their willingness to find employment

Schoolchildren in Mississippi enjoy cookies provided by the Junior Red Cross.

Education suffered as well. Schools were given less money. Many closed. In schools that remained open, older students assisted the teacher. They helped younger children with their work.

Americans were careful about what they spent money on. They only bought **necessities**. The low demand for other items caused even more factories to close.

FUN & GAMES

Many toys during the Great Depression were homemade. Scooters and race cars were often made from orange crates and roller skate wheels. Dolls were made from rags sewn together and scrap buttons. Children took good care of their toys.

Farmers who still owned their farms fared a bit better. They were able to live off their own produce. They traded what they did not need for other supplies. Farmers on the Great Plains, however,

faced a tougher situation. Southwestern states were experiencing one of the worst **droughts** in history. Wind sent dry, loose soil swirling through the air. Soon, the land was useless for farming.

CHAPTER 3

SOUP KITCHENS AND HOOVERVILLES

Soup kitchens sprang up around the country. The poor and hungry waited in lines to be served soup and bread. One soup kitchen in Detroit, Michigan, served up to 3,000 people each day.

A cook prepares soup and bread in New York City.

Herbert Hoover was president from 1929 to 1933. He believed the economy would eventually right itself without more help from the government. Americans were angered by the lack of action, especially those who had lost their homes. With nowhere to go, homeless Americans built shacks in empty lots across the country. They called the little shack towns "Hoovervilles."

A still-growing Hooverville in Seattle, Washington, shown in 1934.

CHAPTER 4

ROOSEVELT AND RECOVERY

President Franklin Delano Roosevelt took office on March 4, 1933. Before this, many banks closed their doors. Fearful Americans took their money out of banks. This caused the nation's banking system to fail. The president's

first task was to deal with the bank **crisis**.
Congress quickly passed a law that
allowed the government to reorganize the
national banks.

On March 12, Roosevelt began addressing the nation through radio broadcasts known as fireside chats. Americans gathered around their radios to listen. Roosevelt carefully explained how banks worked. He reassured the public that banks would be safe when they reopened. Within a few days, Americans began putting their money back in banks.

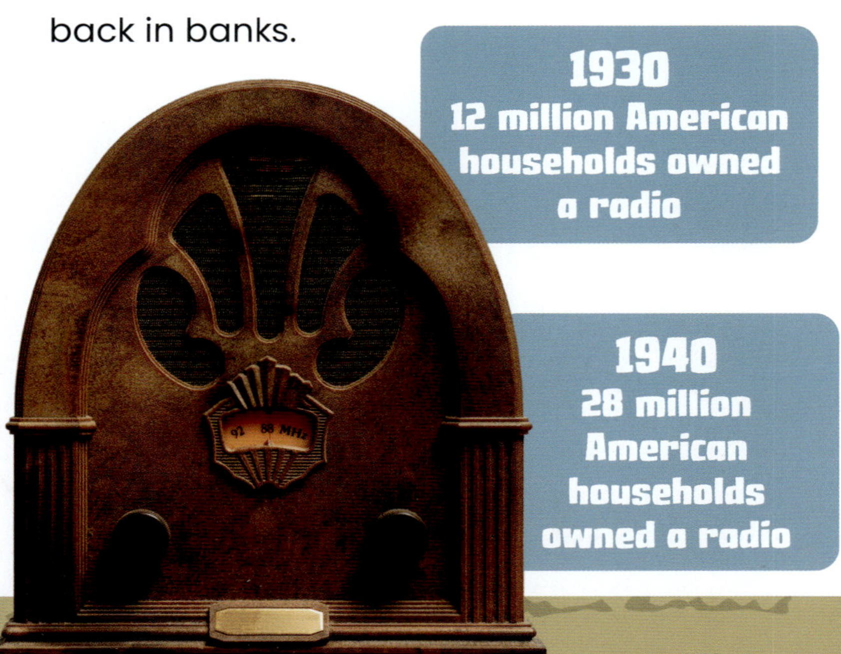

Radios were an
important source of news
and entertainment.

The child of an Oklahoma farmer attends sewing school.

Roosevelt also created government agencies known as New Deal programs. Some programs were later declared unlawful. However, the economy still slightly improved.

Americans remained careful with their money. They mended and reused the items they had or learned to make what they needed. Women would knit and sew clothing at home. Americans threw away very little in case an object could be made into something useful.

People also tried to forget their troubles. Many movies during the Great Depression were lighthearted and full

of music and dancing. Dance studios

became common. People began joining

contests called dance marathons.

A woman in Los Angeles, California, takes part in the Buy In September campaign meant to support Roosevelt's national recovery program.

It took several years, but the United States slowly recovered from the Great Depression. The people of the United States became stronger during this time. This would serve them well in the days ahead. World War II (1939–1945) was looming on the horizon.

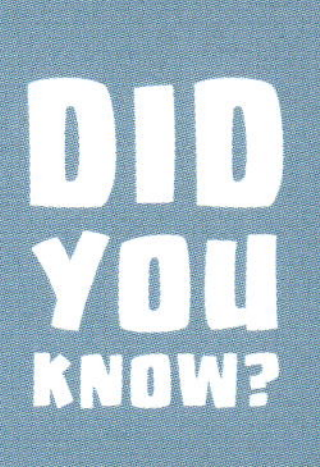

Dance marathons were popular contests for those who were unemployed. Participants were given food and shelter. Winners received cash prizes!

A DAY IN THE LIFE

Andy is a 12-year-old boy who has been sent to live on his grandparents' farm. Andy must stay there until his father finds steady work.

6:00AM

Andy gets up and helps round up the cows for milking. While his grandfather and uncle milk the cows, Andy feeds the workhorses and cleans out their stalls.

7:30AM

Andy washes his face and hands and changes his shirt for school. He eats a breakfast of ham, eggs, and biscuits.

8:00AM

Andy begins his walk to the one-room schoolhouse closest to the farm. Throughout the day, the teacher lectures one grade at a time while the others work on their lessons.

3:00PM

Andy attends a blacksmithing class taught by the local blacksmith. He is learning to mold iron into various shapes. The **WPA** sponsors the class.

4:00PM

Andy arrives home to finish chores with his grandpa and uncle before supper. His grandma is preparing meat, potatoes, onions, and radishes grown on the farm.

7:30PM

After a bath, Andy settles down with his family to listen to the radio. As they listen, Andy's grandfather helps him mend his shoes.

MAKING CONNECTIONS

TEXT-TO-SELF

Imagine that you were alive during the Great Depression. How would your life have changed? Are there any items you own today that you could live without if you had to?

TEXT-TO-TEXT

Have you read any other books about life during the Great Depression? How was the information in that book different from the information in this book?

TEXT-TO-WORLD

What would the world look like if the Great Depression had never happened? What programs wouldn't exist today without Roosevelt's New Deal program?

GLOSSARY

crisis — a situation that is not stable or certain.

discrimination — the unjust treatment of certain groups of people based on characteristics such as race, gender, religion, etc.

drought — a long period with little or no rain.

economic — having to do with the money system of a country, or economy.

export — to send to another country to sell.

loan — money that is lent by a bank that must be repaid with interest.

necessity — a thing that is needed.

stock market — a financial market where investors buy and sell shares of companies.

WPA — short for the Works Progress Administration, a program started in 1935 that employed 8.5 million workers in construction, arts, theater, and literary projects.

INDEX

popbooksonline.com/grt-dep-life

*Scanning QR codes requires a web-enabled smart device with a QR code reader app and a camera.